Notes Drawn from the River of Ecstasy

WILLIAM KISTLER

William Kistler

COUNCIL OAK BOOKS ~ TULSA AND SAN FRANCISCO

The following poems were previously published:

The American Poetry Review, "And Then There Were the Feet" and "Standing Near the Ghats Along the Ganges"

Nimrod, "The Not Found" and "Time Out of Mind"

Pivot, "Slowly, as in Motion"

Poetry Flash, "What Wasn't Seen at the Economic Conference"

Poetry International, "Lines Written About 2 A.M."

Salamander, "Bridge of the City"

In memory of:
DALE HARRIS
MARGOT HEMINGWAY
RAY JOHNSON

with special thanks to:
SANAM

and with salutations to:
PETER BEARD
STEVE BERG
SUSAN BROCKMAN
PATRICIA BURNHAM
SUSSAN DEYHIM
DAVID HATCHETT
RICHARD HOROWITZ
JOYCE JENKINS
ANDY MOSES
DOUG RICE
BARNABY RUHE
PEGGY SHUMAKER
RACHEL WEINTRAUB

GREEN CALLS TO BLACK IN THE NIGHT. . .

CONTENTS

VOYAGE

Penetrating so many secrets
we cease to believe in the unknowable,
but there it sits, nevertheless,
licking its chops.

H. L. Mencken

If you don't break your ropes while you're alive,
do you think ghosts will do it after?
The idea that the soul will join with the ecstatic
just because the body is rotten—that is all fantasy.
What is found now is found then.

Kabir

WHERE THE PAST JOINS THE PRESENT

OUT ON THE EVERYDAY

In the bank are women tellers
In the vault are male counters
As the door turns open
combed-out music lengthens in
Temple of the standing
Temple of the waiting

It is necessary to sing softly
in order to gain Savings

Temple of paper
Temple of records
Harder meat feeds on weak
Numbers feed on beef
To the ordered go
the bonds of the present

What Wasn't Seen at the Economic Conference

Mercury arc lights were shining in the street
where two cigarettes inhaled the day and one
man coughed and the other left for the place
where the jungle was weeping birds and the desert
next door breathed a sigh of extended relief

though there were dark clouds hanging overhead
and the traveler's brushed leather suitcases
fell open, displaying their white shirts.
As the airplane took off I began to applaud,
noticed its streamers of exhaust, walked on.

When at last we ended our stay, I remembered
what Pina said, *We were lovely, we were sweet,*
we were precious little things. On the other
hand, it's possible I follow everything you say
because you have a large mouth and large teeth.

Very well, you agree, but what is the point?
I can't be quite sure, though certainly
we began with two cigarettes. Perhaps
it's the black-coated waiter delivering drinks
in a jungle weeping a rainbow of birds.

LINES WRITTEN ABOUT 2 A.M.

Because we have legs which step forward
we make houses with steps, then we are
above the earth. Stranger in this strange land,

I no longer understand the merchant who hopes
for heat in summer so he can sell fans,
cold, bitter winds in winter so he can sell

heaters. When the four-lane highway appeared
I was already walking. I put on my shoes,
I ran as hard as I could. I got in my car,

I drove as fast as I could. Lagging behind,
I sought books, I thought as deeply as I could.
Someone's words repeated themselves: *Great love*

springs from great love of the beloved object,
and if you little know it you will be able
to love it only a little or not at all.

The large, I see, goes into the larger
and the small into the smaller. Each of us
moves within the size we carry with us.

About 2 A.M., in fact, everything greys
into a haze of pixels and one is left
turning in a reel of fan adverts and tire-

bursting car chases which end at a roadside bar
where a man more handsome than present
is speaking with a sun-drenched heroine

whose eyes suggest she has never had to answer
the call of nature and whose nails remind us
she is waiting to begin a cat-like

tearing of back and faces. Will there ever
be an end to this waking and falling back,
this falling back and rising to wake?

From the Height Where the World Is Seen

Every seat was filled. Some were eating
or looking at statistics on screens
or refiguring the figures of the marketplace.
It seemed that only I needed to look out —
white clouds were forming above broad
stretches of black pine broken by slate-
blue streams. I began to write. When I began

I had nothing to say. When I ended
I was surrounded by many voices speaking
of the profit hunger rising like flame
from within the rooms of the city, drawing
the life printed on faces and the strength
of arms and even the white offerings of food
into their red fire. While, at the same time,

someone handed me a card with a name
known on the other side of the world's ocean,
where that same hunger glistened from shirt
buttons and from the tips of gold pens putting
signatures to the cutting of trees. O northern
forests, dense in white snow and standing
at the last edge of wilderness, breathe your sharp,
needled scents into the angers of my sadness.

Postcard from Beyond I

Between the logician's abstraction of being
and the philosopher's abstraction of nothing
I choose walking. Between lion-like, down-
in-the-gut anger at the harshness which swings
its deft, invisible hand over the human
landscape and calls itself "market freedom,"

and a limitless opening of compassion
toward the abused and the abuser, I choose
all four of her fingers filling my mouth
as she sees I am singing words to her
given to me by leaves turning from light,
first-birth green, to leaves realizing

bottomless black-green. Between a life
devoted to data stored in corporate memories,
and the lightness of the mendicant seeker's
begging bowl, I choose the one small room,
the one meal, allotted the truth-teller. Can
this mind carry these seeming contradictions
in its tangled weave and still walk in gentleness?

Not yet perhaps for me in this lifetime
friend, and many-eyed reader. And so it is
that I am speaking to you from the place
beyond the door which has turned its longing
to the openness of windows through which
light from a sea of unbroken possibility
can be seen to be rolling, rolling.

POSTCARD FROM BEYOND II

I think I remember I entered at about
the place where he said, *Let's put a stop to this
for all time.* It was a very American place.
Bright sun, a short, bare street, four grown men
attempting to take the direction of the world
into their own hands. And what was there they might
have put a stop to? The illusions of the governed?

The desire to profit from the work of others?
Or, on the other hand, the admittedly naive belief
in a single truth, an end to difference? Yes,
and then the phrase, *for all time,* as if there
could be a finish to measuring, to the hungers

of ownership. I do remember there are worlds
in this unbroken universe where time and days
are not a beginning or a month, and one can see
as if across an open sky, a place where
there is no holding anyone hostage to our clock.

Bread not money grows on trees there,
and in the rivers of those valleys, oranges
tumble onto shore, pour their juices straight
into freely open veins. That is the place
of an endless sun going into morning,
into evening, and each can see each life
renewing itself out of the earth of its past,

faces of an original harmonic family arriving
through the endless legs of Goddesses, the endless
arms of Gods, not different from, only more calm
than the way we shape ourselves, such a place
as temple dancers might imagine, step to inhabit.

Dawn in the Charnel Ground:
Brompton Cemetery, London, 1996

So many have "come to rest here." Walking
I ask who are these bones calling out
from within me and who are these bones resting
six feet under me? And on this stone the words,
His Light Shineth. And under layers of ivy
and under scales of moss and under droppings of birds
the carved words are fading. This is a 19th
century cemetery. Many who lie here
worked the decks of the Royal Fleet. Cannon shells,

cats, and cats-o-nine-tails taken to the far
ends of the seas. And who remembers who
was Captain, who the mate, and who the one
who questioned? And what I know is this pen stroke
begins the first thought of the first word
they never spoke. So many stories waited to be told,
as these stones wait to fall over their drying bones.
And even after the gains of empire, nothing
but struggle between person and person.

And now each of us walks on in the continuing
angers of history, fiery in our burning of oxygen,
rich in our carrying of earth's minerals, earth's
salt. And still the question who am I, speaks
from behind these eyes. And who are these Captains
silent amidst the black voices of crows,
silent with the whispered past of Empire,
alone with lives given up to the Union Jack?
What I hear through the veil of years is a calling

from one life of longing to another. I hear.
I answer — *We fill ourselves out in longing.*
Tears do not hold failure. And even the concern
of those who wonder if this walker among stones
which bear but the barest memory of those departed
may somehow break their peace, this is not
to be feared nor the hard-backed beetle tearing
bits of white from the faces of wild roses,
nor the fallen limb loosing its brown tannin
over the date: 1896. We are here in the wash
and sweep of the going on. Longing is our sea.

WHAT IF THE UNIVERSE

What if the universe in its infinite reachings
were no larger than this earth? The imprisonists,
those who have chosen to feel they must control,
would have no further to extend their desires,
their hunger to take each thing into the airless
room of their own hands: as, for instance, land,
water, even those beginners on life's journey —

humans. And whatever the imprisonists can't own
they encase in, for example, cans, like crab,
like salmon, or in iron cages, like bears, lions,
those living who can't make peace with the measuring
of each thing. Pushing. Pushing hard. This
imprisonist society I find myself in is pushing
hard against the wind of the present in order

to own the things of the future — a television
telephone, which, in addition to presenting color
pictures of those then speaking, plays the music
of those who lived before. But what of the past,
my voracious, imprisonist friends? None of it
turned out as you thought, and when it was finished
you couldn't force the historians to keep it straight.

Along the way the image you had worked so hard
to create was lost, and by then you had missed
the sunset which had been set for each of us.
Not simply the orange, fiery kind, but the more
unusual one of lavender, purple, with an upper
wash of azure, such as I saw last night
out of the airplane window. The way in fact

it all turned out, sunsets wound up being
the moment when I could most easily forget
how many the imprisonists have locked in a place
where their bones ache from the scream of being
continually confined, and a single key
sits in the hollowed-out desk of a Court,
and only a Judge who puts on a black robe
and walks on a seamless carpet can intervene.

WHERE THE PAST JOINS THE PRESENT

At least four tongues which I can no longer
blend in my head are speaking from my cell's
memory. And where I began I can no longer
end, and where I think I end I no longer am.

Continue and continue where brake pads release
and cars turn noiselessly in the street,
and the many voices run on into a twittering
as in the trees of birds. Continue and continue
and enough is heard where the shouting

between people is rough and rough-hewn.
It forces my attention further than I intended,
to the point where the bridge is built
over the river and civilization puts its form
on every walking thing. Such a straightening

of the first and living rhythm tests my faith,
my continuing. I am not a believer in what
is called progress, the triumph of the modern,
only the attempt at song. Indeed, I will offer
my voice to the moon at the earliest hour

of seeing. Yes, and I will remember its light
has the long fingers of my life's truest love
and there is now no turning back to youth,
this moon is here as the full moment of the present.

Everyone Who Ever

Everyone who ever had the chance has stepped
on my back. And everyone who could have
has stood on my head. And they weren't

even quite mad, they felt they had to.
In the streets people are asking for money
then turning to drink from the hand

that pushed them down, "the invisible hand,"
which allocates every resource and leaves
the voice of fairness to the readerless

pages of poets. And now I am seeking
a life where work and worker are one,
product and those who produce are one.

The scaffolding of possessions might fall away.
Fear and fear of falling might be given up.
Chords from an ownerless piano would be heard.

The park across the street, indeed,
would receive the shoes holding all the feet,
the feet would feel sure they were part

of the order of the day. My parents would begin
to speak without tumors in the voices
of my children. A free passage between generations

would rise. And meanwhile I am still looking
in the faces of friends for one other one
who might be asking questions. This way out

into the freedom of the unmeasured, the aged
seer says. This door open into distances
of yourself, the tribal dreamer whispers.

LATE SUMMER

Late summer, you ask me why with a heart
as full as the lights of the Northern sky,
I'm loosing tears into the clock ticks of the present,
friends, this is a market selling time
and many of us are twisting our hands
and stepping into sadness as a means of defense.

Friends, I'm looking at the broken stoops
the Congress passed over when they voted
weapons research, and I'm seeing children
born with crack spreading the fitful languor
of those without work down their veins. Friends,

I'm hearing the faster-than-hand firing of Uzis
on each corner of our streets and I am
remembering we promoted democracy with napalm
and destroyed tropical forests with Agent Orange.

Friends, before I paid for a glass of wine
its taste was as sweet as the strings of a violin,
before I paid for a compact disc
I felt the hand beats of the gypsy in my heart,
before I worked in the windowless office
I breathed the grand questions of Beethoven
and drank the elusive, silvery sadness of Mozart.

And now I carry your pots of red lipstick
from room to room, as if I did not hear
the crying of the whales who shed their ambergris into it.

Late summer, my friends, and I'm remembering
nights open to the arms of holding and sea-
washings of love lifting out of them. It seems,
in fact, as if the place where we knew harmony
has shrunk, and while certainly there are
more of us coming into this life there is less
of the joining of friendship between us. Friends,

I am standing up and walking around my desk
in order to look into your faces, while you
ask me to hold back the descent of the sun,
hold onto the day, and I say yes life is short
but let us do something direct, let us plant trees,
protect water, sit down, free the tongues of reason,
renew each field and room connecting us.

California Perfect

How can light be without error
where it falls evenly over the stones?
How can her right leg cross effortlessly
over her left and both be wrapped

in the same flowing copper skin
which also flows over arch, over bone,
and is bound by straps that cross, criss-cross,
hold the soles of sandals to the soles

of her feet? And the lemons of the lemon tree
presenting a full, unblighted yellow.
It is California perfect. Morning
speaks in my ear — you are free,

you are as you know you have been,
free from the standing place of fear,
free from life lived as if in the echoless
tomb of failure. And of course I will

drive from this office, someone's car
will abruptly stop. I will hit him.
Someone else will scream. The man in the car
will pull a gun from the glove compartment.

Everyone will lower their heads. On the floor
the threads of the car mat will be even,
clean, not yet drenched in the blazing
scarlet of this body's perfect blood.

VISITOR'S ROOM, RIKER'S ISLAND

Grey aluminum bands are set at eight inches
where this window looks on a court
whose stones are so evenly cut they seem
factory-produced. Here everything
is measured and put into dimensions
that are hard for people to slide through
or go around. Down and down falling,

white snow falls down through the court,
swirls counterclockwise, and, lifting,
going against gravity, gradually sticks
to ridges in the stone, collecting thicker
here, thinner there, for reasons that seem
random. Patterns of snow falling. Patterns
of snow coming to rest. Silence that is

deep where it rests. Silence in my heart
that is deep where pictures of her person
rise, take the shapes of Goddess, of demon-
destroyer. Was she any one of the people
I thought her to be? She was many people
neither she nor I knew her to be.
Too much strength. Like Cordelia her passions

overcame her. And still the anger of youth
shows in her face at the several voices
speaking loudly and telling their stories
as rapidly as they can. Each visitor
for once is listening. This is a place
where the distance between people is so great
very little of life or energy can be

exchanged. This is a place none of us made
and none in our young days could have imagined.
The distance in my heart is great where
it waits for the moment when she will leave,
walk down halls without windows, through
doors without rooms, opening onto yet other
doors without rooms. There might be rooms

if people lived here, but no one does live here.
People are kept here. Her shoes sound on the floor.
A multitude of voices rise and echo around her.
She is leaving. People are imprisoned here.
The distance between the rooms is very great.
Door metal clangs behind her. Keys repeat her name.
The distance between the sounds is very great.

The Not Found

I can't find it, I still can't see it,
the calm I lived before the hundred hungers
of the city became the need I couldn't finish,
the wall-less room of continuing, night
without darkness, my worn search. And who
is advancing this hunger which has no path,

no direction of imagining? I can't find it,
I still can't see it, the face of the city
which once held the hope of harmony
between citizens. On each corner hands
swell with guns, eyes are feverish. And this
is my hand I am holding in the fire and these

are your thoughts where you stand beside me.
We both are outside looking in and no one
is here to receive us. And who is there
who understands the freedom of passing from this place
which we mark by the setting of the sun,
which we call the life before death, which

we think of as time bound on both sides
by nothingness, as if anything or even
the idea of nothing, could arise out of nothing.
O foolish, crab-like scuttlings of mind
moving across this corner of the limitless flow.
Thinker, reader, I ask you to remember

the long necks of West Africans, the leg strength
of the Masai, our flesh takes whatever form
we imagine. Therefore make no argument
with those around you, our general ignorance
is the work of the mind, anger the fear of not
having enough, greed the defense from fear.

And beyond those defended walls are evenings
of open freedom. Each of us must wake to them
as if we were nameless. There is freedom,
nothing of fame to pose under, nothing
of arrogance to fail out of, only the single
candle on the single table, tongues of a present

without words in the solitary, pulsing night
whose stars are as one with the universe of cells
speaking their rhythms through all the veins of us.

SAGAPONACK BEACH

Almost nothing. This sea which is both
a dark and a light blue depending upon
where the sun strikes it in relation to the eye,
and this sky, more even, more open in its blue
than any framed by a painter, are both

insubstantial, almost nothing, being
as they are, waves of energy passing over
and through one-another. And thus they can
never be the same from moment to moment,
as in the river you step in again and again,

and though it looks the same and speaks the same
whispers of continuing, is not the same,
being higher or lower, muddier or less muddy,
always flowing. Things change as things remain.
The sky that was blue now has a streamer of grey

which is either the front of or the furthest
end of a passing storm. And that grey cloud
is darker than it was one hundred years ago
because of the weight of ash borne to it
by the continuous burning of coal and oil.

And even the 5th Century Greeks cut the trees
from almost all of their archipelago
to build ships, and this left their mountains
looking like the shaved heads of convicts,
and just now a fishing trawler with nylon nets

is dragging all the fish from this sandy shoal
in just the same way, some summers ago,
people went with vacuums to the thin,
gravelly shores of Accebocce Bay and drew
every clam up into bags. It was as if

countless ages of eyes had not held them
freely in their minds, but had drawn them up
one bright morning for the single purpose
of satisfying some rebel hunger. O smoke
from fires which burned their left-over shells,

and smoke from this trawler that is lighter
than that black, coal-smoke which William Turner
shaded into the instinctive colors of fear
as it rose from the first steamships of the 1820s,
no one now among us can turn history back

or wash a century of oil from this beach.
Things change as things remain. Where there
once were trees there are no trees, and where
clams built their fluted shells out of light,
sea water, green algae, there are no clams.

The present we are living in comes to us
bearing the print of the past as it flows on
and as it now will be changed by the shape
of the choices we have made. This is the present
that will be seen in the form of the future.

Poem from a Life Imagined in Prague

These large plane trees stretch away in rows
before me, the faces of their completed leaves
suggesting infinite lives, the voice
of my continuous longing, feeling larger
than this moment. And now the one chair

I sit in, holds the jacket which had been
the emblem of my reaching toward women
when my hands still sang with flowing hunger,
and those days, those glowing salt-semen nights,
felt as full and impassioned as the rays

of the arriving sun. The weight of my own age
has left this voice surrounded in frames
of memory. And still this walking, these trees
standing as if etched in crystalline silence,
then speaking in the phrases of the century

before the tanks came, when the faces of people
and flowers crowded about, opened their red
and orange colors before us. I saw myself
in the clothes of Liszt, inventing the chords
of Chopin, expansive in the life of the spirit,

stalwart in the cause of justice, filled
with the soundings of love. Return to me Muse,
return you lost Romantic longings, only
your charged whispers can reclaim this life
which once stepped into the heights of mountains,

turned, saw itself bound by names, watched,
saw the printing of the calendar of hours,
went on field by eastward field, into
forests of search, believed again that one word
made strong beside another, one hand held out

in an act of hope, could frame a union
between people, that union widen and like
the falling of the round, many-sided moons of rain,
dissolve these measurings of time, of labor,
of those still held within the order of production.

BRIDGE OF THE CITY

Now Walk Before Me

Now walk before me, now stand before me,
the lost company of my life.
Each calls for the bread of blue skies,
for the season of sharing they never had.

And ever-after each is weighed
in the sun of the market place,
each is entered on the ad man's list,
each becomes a silent renter.

And everywhere in the street
there is laughter between polished teeth
when the words of longing or the breasts
of hope are bared. After the first fall

the next goes unnoticed. The day remains,
luminous, a life unto itself.
And on a night in a foreign place
a man thought by himself to be becoming old

is loved so deeply by a stranger
his song comes all the way back to him.

BRIDGE OF THE CITY

City of trade. City where money inverts its face
and claims an arm from every citizen. City
where citizens pass hunger from mouth to mouth,
let many drown in its drying thirst. City of pianos
sounding broadly and calling those sleeping to wake.
City of two exchanging hands as rings of hope.

City of two walking, as we met walking
on a broad bridge over a broad river
with a red sun signaling a night beyond,
signaling light across an ocean dark
with shadows of myriad fish, dark with blood
from a universe of human wars, dark with waste
from the streams of a thousand other swollen cities
poisoning the mother, poisoning the father,
the sister, the primal, plankton-bearing waters.

Over the river the eyes of these two walking.
Over the river rain falling on sunset,
on darkness with its unalterable entering.
Each thought of the moment each might touch the other.
I thought of the light within the moment I might know her.
She thought of the room in which she would know me.
We crossed from one shore to the other.

Sonnet Moderne I
FROM A LINE BY HOWARD BERMAN

She tore her frock off, also removing and removing
her life of unrequited hungers, also removing
her manner's sadness. With everything before her
she chose my hand. Gone. Gone. She was

a long time and what seemed afterward a short time
gone with each part of me. Do not hold. Do not.
I did not hold to her. The one thing she said to me
on that night was — *This is the truest thing*

I will do with you, after this the waterfall
of failure and forgetting. In a tunnel with grey walls
I looked out the rail car window, saw her face
before she had made up in the morning. In the colors

within bottles waited a corner of her life
of going forward, in the words of mind waited mine.

Four Tomatoes

She bent to pick up the newspaper.
Four tomatoes fell from her shopping bag,
landed with soft, almost inaudible sounds
that were like lungs which loose a sigh
once they have folded themselves in.

I felt them on the bare wood as if my own
body also was bruised. Both of us paused,
watching them was like watching a landslide
or some other seemingly inevitable
movement within nature. They rolled, hung

suspended, fell from step to step. They were
before me as separate, then together as one.
Our eyes turned toward each other. Light
from the stairwell passed between the bars
of the banister, passed across our shoulders.

There, in that place, set apart from language
and the restless eyes of others, I sensed
we both were free from holding back.
Round, deeply red, each tomato went on
rolling, falling, rolling again and falling.

After a time we knelt, gathered them in.
The next day she invited me for a drink.
I felt I had been remembered by someone
I had known in an harmonic joining of voices
or some other intense linking of people

where something stronger than ordinary energy
had flowed with seemingly independent weight
over those everyday events we had assumed
we understood. Three tomatoes sat
in her kitchen window. The fourth rested

on her cutting board. Their redness seemed
untroubled, seemed to give off its own light,
called up into a singing, each color lying
hidden within me. In that expanded moment
I no longer felt my life had found its limits,

I saw I had not understood as much of this place
as I had thought. Behind appearance, behind
the mind-imposed order of the expected,
there was the non-order of things arriving
like this and then like that, as if their faces

and shapes were rising limitless out of the well
of becoming. She began to cut the first
tomato. It parted with only its skin giving
resistance. Juice and a gelatinous film of seeds
spilled down the blade, down onto the wood.

I raised my eyes, looked directly at her.
She stopped cutting. What did either of us know
about one with another? Our days had been spent
in the crowd and truck scream of the city.
The room stood open, I was beginning to listen.

SIXTEEN LINES FOR THE POET

Her mouth opened, flame-ends of truth telling
came forth in the layered rhythms of her poem's
life. She did not hesitate, words fell upon words
like coals exploding in a burning building.

I looked into her eyes, they held the place
and time of the unassailable present. I looked
into her face, it held a depth of strength
which went on giving birth. Two days later

my path crossed the sandy bed of an arroyo.
Amber eyes, the fiery brush of a desert fox,
burned in the translucent calm of morning.
I looked in. I looked on in. I saw the flame

of her words announcing the same here of this
same present. My feet lifted. I began to run.
It was a full burning which came forth, legs
giving presence to her eyes. Everywhere their fire.

IMAGINING

It began with her. She said she loved me
when she thought she still loved him.
Then he held to her further, longer.
I couldn't be with her with the shadow
of his unhappiness falling over us.
Secretly I loved Carol. Carol had thought
she loved me, now she found that thought real.

That was where we began—acts of imagining.
Love is imagining. If you give me five days,
I'll give you ten. If you send bronze,
I'll return gold. When she stepped toward
my dying body, passion still held between us.
She went on living and she claimed the robe
of my presence went on surrounding her.

Death wasn't what this body was about then.
Beyond flesh there is more, still more,
the robe of presence is electric, is many-
layered—these words on the pond face
of an open page and sinking deeper, deeper
into it, imagination rising further, wider,
the mind of knowing coming forward.

SONNET MODERNE II

Her face presents itself like a flower at the window,
meeting me whenever I turn. I am in the market,
her eyes continue among the jars, a shining
brought forward as the voice of her senses.

Beside her eyes her hip begins, its curve opens
the memory of the single blond hairs which seemed
to grow in innocence there, which seemed to speak
a burnished calm like the solitude of dawn.

The flame of her face hands itself to me again
and again, like the effulgence of a found harp.
At the place of the green fields her warmth
doubles and redoubles in the brightness of day.

Amidst such abundance my life is no longer
my own. I am an earth to the force of her life,
as full with receiving as the beaches of the sea.

By the River Beyond the City

It's going by faster, she said, than we could
ever have thought, I can't keep the picture.
And deeper, wider the passing of the river's mirror
led us in. Was there a place where this life
began? I see the face of my grandfather's
grandfather as he came from his mother's labor.
Theirs, also, were steps across the rippling waters
of our extended memory. Presence, here, in the midst

of lives past. Presence with no beginning.
Fortunes gained, generations lost, and even
records written by the fire in the winter silence
have faded into the endless stretching back.
And still it's December, and ice casts its widening
circles through these breaths. Was that your full
truth, the mind you opened so broadly before me?
At one moment it seemed a complete release,

and at another a considered presenting. Slowly
we cross the distance hidden in the corridors of words,
slowly we are holding. No agenda and no end.
Each feels he/she is being taken alive
in the arrow-like cell by cell transference
passing between us. In spite of taxes, taxis,
lipstick, hair spray, each is taking the person
of the other into their cell's consciousness,

and even the thousand city voices spinning
contradictions and confusions back over themselves
cannot end the cell's life of connection.
By the river, in the flowing stillness,
we are holding. We lie down in a forest
of night's past, hear the words of tribal memory—
feel beyond ruin, feel this union.

In the Body

This isn't making love, she said, *this is*
being joined in the body of energy and it is
like the rain-fall washing of sorrow when
light suddenly strikes it. Begin. Begin.

How did this begin? We began to feel.
Freedom toward feeling, release from longing,
a door through which one saw the other.
I see her head leaning into and turned

to the side of mine, one of her legs in vertical
counterpoint. I see her head breathing with mine,
from there the teeth of fearless, desert-stalking
hunger coming from the center of her eyes,

from there a long in-pulling. *Let us live*
inside each other, she whispered. So many
voices had spoken. I heard the calm
at the depth of the Temple Goddess whose hundred

arms held every form of sensual conceiving,
I heard the paired arms of the Mother
whose heart held holding, I felt the arms
of the woman bearing vegetables from the rainbow-

mist of the fields, her eyes, her hair, flaring
outward like a fire unbanked in the hearth,
I heard the buyer and I heard the seller,
I heard the agent who framed contracts. Each

of her voices finding its range in the place
where she sought to live within and beside
this separate other. And the further I let myself
open into her, the further she came toward me.

This body as a sun rising to illumine the heavens,
every forest and valley, each energy
and all the copious seas of her, the two of us
as a broad, inextinguishable air of knowing.

SONNET MODERNE III

When she gave me bit by bit the never-told
truths of her life, I wept secretly
as if from joy at the sight of an unexpected shore
appearing in a storm. My heart spread open

as if I had heard the sound of silence
passing through itself—a full, high bell
sounding time and time again down the length
of a courtyard of trees, where, in an imagined

freedom of spring I walk forth, find birds
landing on my shoulders bearing notes
of mystery and revelation. There is no sound

as deep as the rolling through of intimacy
and none as light, like the white heart of the iris
seen now with each of its petals unfolded.

FROM BEYOND

From beyond the divisions of my heart
the sound of your song woke the winds within me
and the hollow of its breath was of the doorways
of stone villages and the gnarled trunks of olive
slopes. Longing, pure, unhindered longing
for the centuries of feet walking beside the stream
beds thick with reeds, beside the waters
passing silently beneath, beside the opalescent
swelling of the moonrise. Place before cities,
before the gases and the hunger of the market
shrugged their almost immobile shoulders at the weight
of bodies throwing themselves from every building.

From beyond the divisions of my heart
the sound of your song brought the wind from the west
bearing a green the color of one's first waking
into green, and then the wind from the south
bearing a red as of the deepest tremors of flesh.
In such doorways of memory, on the arabesque
tiles of such longing, these were the gifts you left.
On this page I pass them back to you,
everything received in living must be passed on.
And first I thank the wind in my heart bearing warmth,
and next I thank the wind of hope bearing
laughter like a free and long-striding daughter.

And finally I thank the wind from the east
bearing the hundred languorous kisses
I would spread upon your back. Yes, and afterward
I thank the wind which does not meet me in the face
but rises from within and draws me into caves
which hold the shapes of each of your songs
not yet sung, and light from the rooms of your heart
where they are broad with knowing, and fire
from your unbound thoughts which reach deeper
than even the azure length of your fingers.

LIFE OF TWO

The way it was between the two of us,
that feeling of union continually
finding the face of its renewing, it was like
a stream bringing the running weight of water

to the depth of a mountain lake. The way
that was, it was never far off, was
never much said, mainly was coming in,
kept coming in, as if the two of us

were merely travelers through the skin
of our lives and had been set down here
to watch the filling out of something
larger. The way that was, it was

finally very strong, came very far in,
so that words acted simply as signs
which flared and fell through the rooms
our lives had stepped into, found open.

If you begin I will improvise. If
you lift your head I will lower mine.
If you cry I will speak in the sounds
of a language not yet imagined.

When We Stand, When We Dream

When we stand, when we step into dance,
you put so much of woman in front of me
I am drawn and drawn in. And because
your feet tilt upward at the harsh angle

of a penitent's eyes, and because lipstick
makes an open clearing in the leafy
forest of your face, and because the rolling
ocean waves of your chest breathe then retract

like a swift-running tide running full,
and because I find myself lit by the white
force of your legs which speak laughter,
speak anger, at once together, at once apart,

I now can feel a river depth of hunger
standing motionless at the center of your longing.
Only a touch formed by hands can bring peace.
And because my hands are as deep with whispers

as the winter black of the northern seas,
and because I step left, step right,
and am always present, you now step toward me
in a passionate turning toward the measure

of your own rhythm. Now, from within the shifting
sighs of rhumba I hear unborn voices calling
at the doors of your ribs, asking for birth.
Women are birth. And I must be alive at a place

somewhere within you where shores of blood
bathe unborn eyes and where I can feel
the wash of amniotic song carrying the need
which marks the end of this man's freedom.

Now, this is when you take me into yourself,
the eye and the eye of the necessity with which
the blood drives forward, igniting the force
that leads to the channel of birth. Now, this

is the soul's journey into the place of life,
this is where heart and blood unite to shape
the colors of creation, this is when a fugue
known only in fingers plays upon the strings

of my back and your voice insists we step
into the heart of our dreams. Now, this is
the moment we depart and this is the moment
we forget such dreams must end in the order

of white picket fences through which morning
glories are calmly growing and beside which
a blue Ford station wagon sits with two small
heads laughing uproariously and looking out.

SONNET MODERNE IV

A guitar, hands lifting chords of passion
like dark birds from its strings. A table,
wine the color of a longing deeper than blood.
Her face which once was purer to him than dreams

is now the ridged face of a woman made older
by death and children. This man, this woman
arrive at the simplest thing—how was it
they left each other? Could he borrow her eyes,

hold them in the place of waking, in the place
of lost days? Between this eternity of remembering
and that act in time he would choose a room
where each part of her might bit by bit be found.

Will it bless him this longing called life?
Will it kill him this parting called love?

As Lived as Life

Heat, and the day holding a weight of bees
and other light-winged flying creatures.
Beside the liquid, stone-face of the pond
I bend in color I think of as flower, gather
the curving faces of anemones to me
as the sky bends deep into nothing.

I ask nothing. Nothing of trees,
how they are spreading. Nothing of blue,
how it is seamless and without speech.
And now you are gone and now I am distant,
and our words stand as they were, as alive
as the leaves and reaching—over the water,

through the blooms, reaching the seeming
continuity of the presence of us.
There is no destruction, no defeat, simply
the past thronging as swallows at dawn.
And carved clear from the folds of memory,
this door opening and going off, going

down where images of our life have been.
Limbs adding dimension, rooms adding light,
your eyes as mind. Hold, and I hold.
Burn, and I burn. Merge, and I am in.
There is no destruction, no defeat,
and where we began we now have gone—

my arm going over your shoulder beside
the events of living. We are as we were,
worn through together and drawn apart.
You stepping from our life into desire,
broader house, more of people, life of power,
myself drifting toward a life of thought.

We are living in the time of trade,
everything must turn over, reform itself,
change. The past surrounds inside me
as I bend and cut. Again it is the summer-
high surge of light. Green, sheer, dragon-
fly wings beating. Water smooth in pools.

Heart the one fact forever which burns
and yet remains. Heart which seems as if
it were all of me. Heart steeped in flame.

ELEGY AT EVENING

At evening, at the moment before the moon
rises and fills the darkness with its one
broad silvery breath stolen from the cave
where the eye of morning sleeps; at evening,
when the light in the water is the light
left after the sun has gone behind the hill,
become a light so pale only water can receive;
at evening, when light holds the glowing

transparent sadness of the place in my life
where you once were, and that sadness calls out
as if understanding itself for the first time,
and there is yet no redeeming of the past,
and just a little way west you are sitting
beside a stream where light also has fallen
wondering if the sadness is in the water
or somehow coded into ourselves and therefore

irreversible; at evening, when earth and sky
open as one mouth, swallow light all the way down,
there time begins, your counting until the moon
knows itself as full, until its light comes
forward, shines with the clearness of first
memory. There, in a length deeper than clocks,
each waits until each can look again
into the shadowed face of the other, in a binding

that heals, at the edge of the hills, under
the trees, free in this light which whispers
peace as the state each of us seeks.
There, at evening, when light turns to shade
and shade spreads its rolling particled waves
into union with the planes of water,
there, each turns, expecting to see the other,
sees themselves alone, standing, looking in.

MEMORY ETCHED IN THE AMBER OF MY LIFE

The deep, the rich, the living remembered maroon
of your lost form lowers itself into me, slowly
takes the light blue of this moment of peace
into its center, spreads out at its edges

into an adjacent orange. From there a falling
into space, a fear of disappearance,
the furthest grey strands of your hair flecked
with a simple red, holding touches of green

suggesting rebirth, a beginning again, a near-in
rhythm of breath which might wake at any moment,
enter into a broad presence within me.
The dark red of you which lingers at the last,

swallows itself until it begins to flow,
holds earth, air, fire, inevitably water,
becomes the shifting, fully staurated,
never before seen, amber ground of my life.

When it fades, departs, I ask myself if it
ever existed, I find myself standing in rain
waiting for clouds to clear, thinking halos
of light passing in mist will release it.

Sometimes at night, holding the memory
of your head tilting back in my hand, the ease
of your unfettered freedom, it comes forth,
overtakes me, the full cavern depth of its warmth

claiming my eyes as the flow of my own blood
is lifted upward, covers all longing,
the features particular to each of us which
I can see I am just beginning to recover.

SONNET MODERNE V

Out over myself you/I turned me,
out from the compliance of sheets,
from the living dark gathered in your hair.
All the way over myself the blood

between us turned, and where it lifted
there in freedom were the lines of your hands,
the shape of your mind, the beginning
and the walking in hunger of your heart.

Walking in, walking always into me.
I believed I had measured my own ends.
I knew only ends, not this moment
which creates a remembering without end.

Yours is the deepest, the broadest face,
I ever saw my full face in.

VOYAGE

Now

Alive in the lake of the nameless,
nameless in the lake of the living,
living in the eye beyond the lake,
printed white.

And Then There Were the Feet

And then there were the feet
showing their white bones beneath the long skirts,
and then there were the these and the and these,
such as the eyes behind the glasses

and the words of the mind behind the eyes
burning and attaching themselves to each thing
before the eyes, which also were burning
and becoming the life freed. And now

I'm off to hear the up and the down
of the unfolded wings of music where they lift
from the strings of instruments. And now
I'm at the station of trains where wheels

go turning through shrouds of steam and the sound
of iron rolling. Such a world is opening
its events before me. And my eyes are only
just beginning to see what they eat, and already

I am anxiously waiting for the sun to set
so that as in the many places and times
of lives past I can hold that fierce burning
out from the darkening body of evening.

THE DOOR WHICH SPEAKS TO THE WINDOW

You, my vision, my window,
are never without the friendship of light,
even if it is the faceless light
that comes to us from unfinished distances,

the wordless light that gives itself
to the stranded fabric of the chair,
bleaches each color, spreads in one breath
and enters all of it, that light

which knows itself within motion, which
stays into winter and remains as darkness,
as the long, drawn out, restorative
floor of darkness. You, my seamless

eye of sight, my knowing of those things
I might never have known, the forking
feathers of birds where they spread
among the wings of leaves, the black

arm of the branch breaking at the moment
when the metal ax of the humans arrives.
You, my single eye, would not know of me
if it were not for the evenness

of these walls which transmit the shudders
of closing, the swinging out and release
of being open. I would not know of you
if it were not for the coming of shadow,

for the knocking-knocking of evening's hand
on the panels of my wooden sight
where I stand in this place of change,
which stands itself from moment to moment

and blinks with change, as I am held
yet feel myself light, unhindered,
surrounded in these hinges by this swirling
curve and river smoke of living time.

MEDITATION

From each different face a different sound,
and each hand held at a different height
is asking for peace differently. Standing up,
sitting down, each person is within the timeless
space of time being. Beginning where we are

we are in the middle of life, neither beyond
young nor before dead, a kind of release
that we remember as freedom. And perhaps
the place of freedom is the space one has
no need to go out from. I do not try
for release, and I do not accept an answer—

one cannot become a little free, as in
the moment when the mind embraces an idea.
And is there a color embodying freedom?
And is that color the same red as for
this breathing self, or is it the almost
transparent white of the timeless? I am

always choosing a red tie, red socks, so
it is clear that the force of the blood's speech
is still within me. Black might be such a color
if anger and dread did not unmask themselves
in the darkest of the dark hours. And it
would seem that out of the well of black, fear

is continually rising. Black is the room
holding the belief in the finality of death.
And now I draw a line under these words
and I understand I am irrevocably tied
to the red of myself. From within the depth
of that reaching I have written on these walls.

First Blue Was There

First blue was there, then the first
bright point within it, like a word
rising out of the not-ever of silence.

Blue deepened, grew black. Then more,
many more bright points came forward,
became a gentle, long streaming
like foam off the washing of a sea,

like a milky singing let forth
to walk as a way across the night.
Fingers of cloud came into the blackness,
covered the streaming. Every sort of braiding

between the depths of far-distant space
and the nearness of cloud began—revealed
themselves as openings, closings, faces,
lengths. Then the wonder in my heart

at things so far off and so mysterious,
in a sky already covered with names—
Andromeda, Cassiopeia, The Bowman—
became a speaking I let go free

into the steps of change. There could
be no finish, only blackness again,
and the continuing of the continuous,
and the milky singing. Yes, and the remembering

of the palms and fingers of white clouds,
as close and floating as those of that departed one
whose hands were always new to this skin.

Brightness

When fire rose from the wood and began
to speak in its quick and crackling voice
I knew my life had brought me to the edge
of this line-smooth lake so that sleep
could realize itself as a living state,
transmit energy into every dream at once.

I lay down. When I woke, all the elements
above the earth had formed a seamless blue
clearer than the blue my eyes reflected back,
clearer than any I had known. I turned
to where the lake held up its heart of water
like the center of a memory. I would not see

that place in that light again, nor the green
path under the trees holding pools of rain
like luminescent flowers. Now, in the midst
of that same brightness, lights are coming on
and glowing in the walled rooms of the city.
I see her eyes open. I see her remember

that, as in a dream without end, she must
walk north up a rise which once was a sacred
tribal burial ground, then east down a slope
which formed the bank of a stream, to a place
where many eyes stare without blinking
into numbers floating on screens. She knows

she is one of those who shape transactions
that determine which among them will own
the things of the city, even the carpet
they will be standing on. Hers is the day
that will be divided into units, and those
are the minds that will do the dividing.

While further on east the river rolls
to its meeting with the sea and does not speak
the name of the Captain who was the first
from another continent to see it. There is
no part of this, I understand, which anyone
can truly own. And though we put our names

everywhere upon it we live in a field
where each thing rises and grows brighter
until it dims and grows darker. Nothing
can be taken away, things only fall
from what they were, like the fading of power,
the end of friendship, or, at another time,

in another place, a rebirth and a shifting
to the side, as in Cezanne's turning of the head
to alter his perspective. Now I stand, look
everywhere about, the waters of the lake seeming
to be a perfect, open mirror I might step
all the way into. Now the white, curled blooms

of wild roses come into view beyond the oak
whose trunk has broadened year after year,
finally is larger than the circle of my arms,
though its leaves still come forth in the fresh,
light-green brightness of a seedling, announce
another corner of the page of original spring.

SLOWLY, AS IN MOTION

And slowly the sound of rung bells
began to rise from their hands, and slowly
from the pouring of their breaths

through the chambered wood of flutes
blown sounds began to rise. They climbed
past large stones and gnarled, stunted pine

bent darker than the hand of night
clear over themselves, and for whom
the blood of time was continuously being felt

as the flowing of wind around them. They climbed,
their sounds blended into the starry going
away of blackness, which, with a calm

written into the curve of the crescent moon,
received them. Their legs walked higher
and easily higher, they were giving

themselves like open water to peace.
And slowly as in the joining of all hope,
they stilled their instruments, the cycle

of their breaths coming quietly fuller,
gently deeper, until the last and the last
of the going away of night was in them,

and being was in walking, was in long breath.

HOPE
FOR THE BALANESCU QUARTET

Thank you my friends, my dear friends,
carrying your four stringed instruments
to the ends of this earth and playing

the last yards and the last feet and even
the single inches of your fullest feeling.
You lifted me from anger, you pulled me down

from the continuous turning of the wheel
of sadness that I was drawn into
when I saw the harsh state of our condition—

hands waiting for coins, other hands
waiting for the shoes of those then sleeping.
You lead me out of rooms which present

voices talking in untruths and wearing
arrogance as the head piece of a shield.
I place my life beside yours. In the clear

light of the furthest corner of the strength
you have illumined, I am where you are,
you are where I am, we are awake

in the flowing river of sunrises and sunsets.

WORDS FROM THE COMPOSER
ALEXANDER BALANESCU

Thank you my friends, my dear friends,
I only play this music for you,
I only take my meals and bathe in it and walk
where it is in thought of you. I only

carry it in my jacket and take it out
where you are. You are part of me. And where
your hands are burned when you lift them
from the sealed oven of the state, and where

your face is lined with fear of the tanks
of the Soviets and of the lengthening
work week of those who exploit your labor
and call it capitalism, and where power

prints its legal code with bullets
along the festering needle marks of your arms
and you fall into the dream of escape,
there your freedom to stand as one will begin.

I turn this music into hope that you will begin.
I turn it into belief in each of you,
into notes which pronounce your long, unwashed hair
and the hurtling chords of your dark Romanian eyes.

Someone Knocked and Looked In

Someone knocked and looked in. It was in
a station at night in the midst of an almost
hopeless darkness. It was in a city
where tall buildings held such darkness
like a life buried up to its arms in sadness.
It was in a nation which enshrined ignorance
as an altar raised on a plain between two oceans.
Someone knocked and looked in. It was in
the midst of an almost disappearing appearance.
Someone brought light. Someone set up cameras.
Doors were opened to the movement of actors.
The scene opened onto tears of love lost.

Tears of a man thought dead in a far off place.
Tears of a woman consoling him whose love
she cannot now return. Tears of a brother
leading the lost man off, as the crowd
holds its breath in the single split-open
note of parting, where the trumpet player
plays an inconsolable lament from the place
within each of their longings, as the camera
pulls away like an eye slowly closing, as
the lights which had been set up for the players
are seen as lights surrounded by a night
gorged full with failure. A corner of a station

where a timeless, insoluble human drama
has taken place without a cinematic ending,
without an all-encompassing, silver-screen
embrace. And as darkness closes further in
and the place of light becomes a distant dot,
you see opening as if from a light lighting
inside yourself, the dream of a white beginning
and birds passing shadowy among the brightness
of leaves which do not yet depart, which
stand shimmering, changeless as pure form,
and this is the place of our mind's imagining
and this now is the light of going forward.

SETTING OUT TO CHANGE,
THEN GOING ON

With this pen stroke I begin again,
seeking to depart from this love of language,
flowing meters, which in their fullest voice
hoped to express the linked and interwoven,
all of one skin, body of the worn, now
born again, now tottering old or walking
upright, day in, day out passage of this life.

Here I begin, not as I might wish
within the clearest place of myself,
not in a fire-cleansed simplicity of words
which might congeal immediately into truth—
a painting painted in blood, a roof form,
a bed on which a death is stretched—but
in this abundance I cannot escape, cannot

ignore, these emanations of thought I take
on and off, these layers of words I embrace
as expression of the flooding river, the expanded
ocean of choice joining the endless sky
within this life like a state of mind that I
am almost always taken to, cannot finish,
cannot end, fate's abundance. My own fullness

discovers itself here, not in the mind of less
is more, but in a fertile, peopled beginning.
The strength of being one connected to many
is alive here. Write it down. This page is what
I know as freedom, here is the broad scaffolding
of event, dissolving into words, into faces,
into the forested mountainside of memory.

ALONE

As I look at every woman with pure, pale skin
I see desire has passed from me. As I
stand with feet placed in the frustration
of the privileged, throw a chair then another,
the largest chair left in the universe,

out of a nearby window, I feel I can no longer
lift myself toward the mind, the life-
essence of another. Belief has passed from me,
is far off, marks itself as the distant
terrain of the young which I once dwelt in.

As I think of the living presence of the women
I have known, each standing like a separate tree
in the valley of the mind, each of which
I might have passed more time with, yet more time,
each now with children, an order of some sort,

moments from the past come forward, present
the bright horizons of first one then another
pair of eyes. She crossed the room, sat down
on the clumped muscles of my thighs, put her arm
over my shoulder. A rustling as of a fresh wind

passing in leaves came over us. Each was filled
with the deep as the depth of night, breath
of the other. Now I am surrounded in a word-
flooding of sound and I call even memory
a distraction, when, flocking and grouping around me

these fierce, expansive words called poetry
descend toward me in clusters like birds, all
piping at once and crowding into the house
of imagining. Is it true that the secret,
evolving life of vision and language only

admits one voice then a second, almost never
the broken strands of daily conversation
bent across and over each other? My friend,
age thirty-five, read his poems with ageless eyes,
made music which resonated with the dream-like

calling forward of freedom. Twenty years later
when I took his hand he held a cane, could
barely stand, said he had stood too close
to the burning tablets of words, had found
they consumed the faces of those around him.

As need passes, feels far off, I feel as if
I had taken myself to a small hut half-way up
a forgotten mountain. No travelers pass there.
I am alone. I have chosen to be alone,
or, rather, those words have demanded silence,

as if the presence of even one other voice
might crowd them out. No longer the wrapping
through of fingers, the waking with the eyes
of another. No longer release from the chiming

of the clock of solitude. Listen, self, hear
your own cadences, their force brings longing
from within. Now I am taken into each moment
of life lived before. I am rocked and held, enter
the place of each woman's spirit, hold no weight.

Alone without the heart-driven beating
of another's breath, I am haunted by faces,
by the curved fingers of hands where they float
before me on the plain of living memory.

Alone with visions from the many-voiced muse
who whispers longing continuously into the veils
of my speaking, alone under the arms of great
summer trees, I am turned over daily, turned
nightly, by the rustling of that one word—alone.

TOMATO

That it should come up heavy, red,
out of a green root, up bearing juice
straight from the rock and soil of earth,

this I can but partly understand, ask myself
if I have the strength to make images as raw,
as natural as this. Now these teeth

take the thin, seed-rich tissue across
their bone-white ends, crush it into
an essence I can eat. Now each organ

turns it through itself, separates it into
its several parts. Now this cavern of intestines
becomes an interment ground for its woven

fibers, and my stomach in each veil
of its hunger, breathes, and receiving
the dense fruit, expands. Look inward

open eye, upon these teeth, this eater.
See also the change and station of the eaten,
these two now walk about as one.

TIME OUT OF MIND

On my way to yet another place,
still calling myself Kistler, this mind
without a beginning (unless you count

birth which is but one face), without
an end, which also is but one moment,
therefore without anything, without any,

without even a. Free in the street,
free in the turnings of the stream,
having forgotten to count. Left entering

evening after evening of light, left
singing of them later as if each were
a speaking which could not be remembered

so would need to begin again, would call
out its life in color as though in rapture,
display its hands, its eyes, then bathe

itself through with streams of sight, come back
across a darkness and a day it might seem
it had held continuously inside.

After Leaving Victor Hugo's House

Under the arched Renaissance columns
of the Place Des Vosges, a man with eyes
looking long into memories unending
was playing Spanish Études on a worn
wooden guitar. High up on a smoke-

blackened wall, in tones of deeper black
was written: *I think through all the days*
of those no longer present — my lost loves.
Frances, Kate, Andra who here remains,

I wish each of you truth unfinished,
a room of space open to dreams, chords
of beginning, arpeggios of change, all
other phases of this ashen moon which now

seems as if it were about to be taken down
into the streets of this city. It is here
that windows shine like eyes filled
with insatiable hunger, hold each of us

fixed, trying to reach to one another.
I, myself, quiet as you remember,
and with every sense heightened by the chords
sounding from behind, still walk on, extend

these words to you as I broaden their rhythm,
as the sound of the guitar fades, is too
far off to be heard, as I am alone as I am,
as you are just as I know you are.

STANDING NEAR THE GHATS
ALONG THE GANGES

Since this is the circumstance of life
and therefore a standing up and a walking
around the corner in order to see

where you are, if you then are in the wrong
place at the wrong time you will likely
be caught between opposing forces

or left alone altogether, either of which
can begin to feel closed in, restricted,
like a kind of death, though daily

these same seemingly inevitable structures
shift and it is possible to see them
as unweighted, uneven, leaving you free

to step from the shores of the nearby stream.
And are we not standing in the waters
of the many rivers? And who is it, friend,

and sometimes ghostly lover, who is standing?
I see that you also are a flowing over,
just as the burning of the dead body

is here a flame of bright anguish,
brought forward, then cracking, bursting
into ash, gone without hesitation

into the sky of continuous beginning.

RETURN

Before I was dead I was old. Before
I was old I ate from a fork and sought
the longing of women. Now the mind turns
slowly away, these cells disengage, forgetting
they once knew the full range of themselves.
And if there had been no love woven through,
there would not have been this feeling
of being borne up, there would have been
only the death of seemingly impenetrable rock.

This is not the death of being lost
in the illusory, imagined realm of nothingness,
of drying bones sealed from earth in concrete tombs.
You cannot fall from the numberless rooms
of this universe. This is the death of coming awake.
The curved dorsal fins of dolphins lead me on.
The charged eyes of each of my ancestral mothers,
fathers, speak through the length of this gene print.

Here is the water of transbirth, change,
the next entering of the next life, the open
windows and airy curtains of a house in which
you are able to see yourself brought head-first
into a narrow, streaming passage, eyes closed
and coming into life as if new-arrived
from the far-off heights of a mountain pass.

VOYAGE

The sun now is light unhindered and the clouds
are flecked with red where they curve to end.
I am aboard the aircraft largest beside
towers and bridges of iron. Jet trails
fade behind, the moon in quarter grows close,
its mountains clearer than the earth's.

One house from the history of my life comes
forward to fill the bare, white wall of memory
standing open inside me, a place where
a stream had flowed with the evenness of blood
through the almost spoken silence of stone.

There I would pause in the last, languorous
light of evening, dream of this height
that I might see. One hour, six hundred miles.
I step from between blankets and magazines,
up the aisles past the sleeping, up the stairs

to the open observation. First stars
are coming into sight on the cobalt blue
glass of the sky. My eyes widen, widen further,
we are earthmen freed into this bound-open
river of living. This flight is not the one flight

and these skies are not the only skies. Somewhere
smoke is pouring directly into smoke,
gas, space, liquid and light are combining
as new and turbulent chemical roses are sewn.
Hands without bones are reaching through
their own energy poles where shifting

spectral windows open. Dense modes,
deeper than light, draw in gravity and time.
Seasons are excised. Eyes flick wide and just
as soon go out. Other earth, other heavens,
on another side of seeking, form and assert

themselves. There is no certainty, nothing
is explained, each thing turns irrevocably
in the taking. Home, immeasurable and open
across galaxe distances and light floes, whole
shape warps, place gone before and waiting

after, where in another form, on another wave,
we were born and have been, born, and in some
unseen future will be. Home, this distant,
stretched out, freedom of the astral seas,
breathing and gathering as if in dream.

William Kistler is a past president of Poets and Writers, and was a founding member of Poets House.

He is the author of three volumes of poetry: *The Elizabeth Sequence,* which won the Oklahoma Book Award in 1989, *America February* (1991), and *Poems of the Known World* (1995). Individual poems have been published in *Antaeus, Harpers, New Directions, Poetry Flash, Poetry International, The American Poetry Review, The New Criterion* and numerous other magazines. In 1992, he co-edited and wrote the lead essay for *Buying America Back,* a collection of essays on America's social and economic problems.